Uranium

and the Rare Earth Metals

THE
PERIODIC
TABLE

Nigel Saunders

Heinemann Library
Chicago, Illinois

Customer Service 888-454-2279

Visit our website at www.heinemannlibrary.com

Design: Ian Winton
Illustrations: Stefan Chabluk
Picture Research: Vashti Gwynn
Originated by Ambassador Litho Ltd.
Printed and bound in China by
South China Printing Company

08 07 06 05 04
10 9 8 7 6 5 4 3 2 1

**Library of Congress Cataloging-in-Publication
Data**

Saunders, N. (Nigel)
  Uranium and the rare earth metals / Nigel
Saunders.
      v. cm. -- (The periodic table)
Includes bibliographical references and index.
Contents: Elements and atomic structure -- The
periodic table, the lanthanides, and actinides --
The lanthanides -- Lanthanum, cerium, and the
twins -- More members of the lanthanides -- The
actinides and radioactivity -- The artificial actinides
-- Find out more.
  ISBN 1-4034-1666-4 (HC), 1-4034-5500-7 (Pbk.)
  1. Uranium alloys--Juvenile literature. 2. Rare
earth metals--Juvenile literature. [1. Uranium
alloys. 2. Rare earth metals. 3. Metals. 4. Chemical
elements.] I. Title. II. Series.
  QD137.U73S28 2003
  546'.41--dc21
                        2003010226

Acknowledgments
The author and publishers are grateful to the
following for permission to reproduce copyright
material:
p. 4 D. Boone/Corbis; p. 10 Roberto De
Gugliemo/Science Photo Library; p. 13 Ariel
Skelley/Corbis; pp. 15, 30 Roger Ressmeyer/Corbis;
p. 16 Lester Lefkowitz/Corbis; p. 19 Jose Luis
Pelacez; Corbis; p. 21 Maximillian Stock
Ltd./Science Photo Library; p. 23 Mark E.
Gibson/Corbis; p. 24 Geoff Tomkinson/Science
Photo Library; p. 25 Getty Images; p. 27 Custom
Medical Stock Photo/Science Photo Library; p. 28
Carl Schmidt-Luchs/Science Photo Library; p. 31
Wellcome Department of Cognitive
Neurology/Science Photo Library; p. 34 Murray
Robertson; p. 36 TWI Ltd.; pp. 38, 49 David
Ducross/Science Photo Library; pp. 40, 43 Michael
Boys/Corbis; p. 45 Yann Arthus-Bertrand/Corbis;
p. 47 Jim Sugar Photography/Corbis; p. 51 Charles
O'Rear/Corbis; p. 53 NASA/Science Photo Library;
p. 55 (bottom) Corbis; p. 55 (top) U.S. Department
of Energy/Science Photo Library; p. 56
Bettmann/Corbis; p. 57 Corbis.

Cover photograph of uranium reproduced with
permission of Corbis.

The author would like to thank Angela, Kathryn,
David and Jean for all their help and support.
Special thanks to Theodore Dolter for his review of
this book.

Disclaimer
All the Internet addresses (URLs) given in this
book were valid at the time of going to press.
However, due to the dynamic nature of the
Internet, some addresses may have changed, or
sites may have ceased to exist since publication.
While the author and publishers regret any
inconvenience this may cause readers, no
responsibility for any such changes can be
accepted by either author or the publishers.

Contents

Chapter 1 **Elements and Atomic Structure** 4

Chapter 2 **The Periodic Table, the Lanthanides, and the Actinides** 6

Chapter 3 **The Lanthanides** 8
From Ore to Metal 10

Chapter 4 **Lanthanum, Cerium, and the Twins** . . .12
Cerium .14
Cerium oxide 16
Praseodymium 18

Chapter 5 **More Members of the Lanthanides** 20
Europium 22
Gadolinium 24
Dysprosium 26
Erbium .28
Ytterbium 30

Chapter 6 **The Actinides and Radioactivity** 32
Actinium 34
Thorium 36
Protactinium 38
Uranium 40
Uses of uranium 42
Bombs and reactors 44

Chapter 7 **The Artificial Actinides** 46
Plutonium 48
Americium 50
Curium .52
Californium 54
Mendelevium 56

Find Out More About the F Block Metals 58

Timeline 61

Glossary 62

Further Reading and Useful Websites 63

Index 64

CHAPTER 1

Elements and Atomic Structure

Everywhere you look there are different substances. Some of them are gases, such as air; others are liquids, such as water; but most of them are solids, such as metals, plastics, and the paper that makes this book. There are millions of different substances, but they are all made from simple components, namely elements.

▲
Everything at this fair, including the rides, stalls, and people, is made from some of the millions of substances in the world.

Elements and compounds

Elements are substances that cannot be broken down into a simpler substance by using chemical reactions. About 90 elements exist in nature. Scientists have learned how to make more than 20 more using nuclear reactions, including 11 of the actinides. About three-quarters of the elements are metals, such as lanthanum, and the rest are nonmetals, such as chlorine. Elements join in countless different ways in chemical reactions to make compounds. An example of compound formation is when lanthanum and chlorine react to make lanthanum chloride. Most substances in the world are compounds, made up of two or more elements that are joined chemically.

Atoms

Every substance, whether it is an element or a compound, is made up of tiny particles called atoms. An element is made up of just one type of atom, whereas compounds are made from two or more types of atoms joined together. Single atoms are far too tiny for people to see, even with a microscope. If you could stack 5 million lanthanide atoms, which are all of a similar size, on top of one another, the pile would only be about 1 millimeter (0.04 inch) high!

Subatomic particles

Scientists once thought that atoms were the smallest things in the universe. They now know that atoms are made from even tinier objects called subatomic particles. Neutrons and protons are joined in the center of the atom to make its nucleus. Neutrons do not have an electrical charge, but protons are positively charged. Electrons are subatomic particles that are even smaller than protons and neutrons and are negatively charged. The electrons are arranged around the nucleus in different shells, similar to the way planets are arranged around the Sun. In fact most of an atom is empty space.

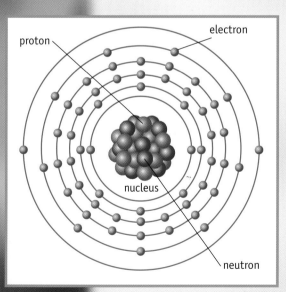

proton

electron

nucleus

neutron

This is a model of a lanthanum atom. Each lanthanum atom contains 57 protons and 82 neutrons, with 57 electrons arranged in 6 shells, or energy levels, around the nucleus.

Groups

Elements react in different ways, which makes chemistry both exciting and puzzling. Several attempts were made to organize them, but Dimitri Mendeleev, a Russian chemist, was the most successful. His table, which he completed in 1869, organized similar elements into one of eight groups, making it far easier for chemists to predict how they might behave. Mendeleev's table was so successful that the modern periodic table is based on it.

The Periodic Table, the Lanthanides, and the Actinides

The modern periodic table originates from Mendeleev's table. The elements are arranged in horizontal rows called periods, with the atomic number (number of protons in the nucleus) increasing from left to right. Each vertical column in the periodic table is called a group, and the elements in a group share similar chemical properties. There are eighteen groups altogether.

The number of electrons in an atom of an element and how they are arranged in their shells determines the way that element reacts. All the elements in a group have the same number of electrons in the shell farthest from the nucleus, called the outer shell. For example, the elements in group 2

▼ This is the periodic table of the elements. The lanthanides and actinides are two series of similar metals, each series containing fifteen elements.

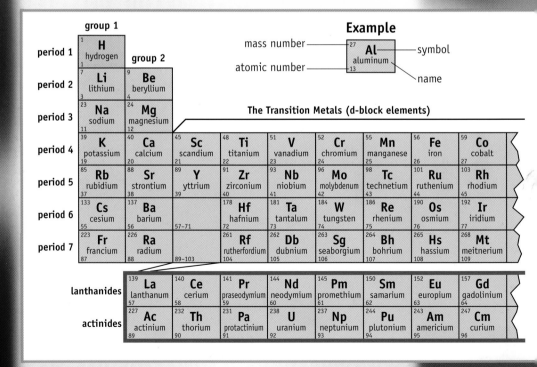

are metals with two electrons in their outer shells. The elements in group have seven electrons in their outer shells. The elements in both groups react quickly with other substances. The periodic table gets its name because the elements are arranged so that their chemical properties occur regularly or periodically.

The properties of the elements change gradually as you go down a group. The elements in group 18, for example, become denser. Balloons filled with helium (at the top of the group) rise quickly into the air, whereas balloons filled with xenon, from near the bottom of the group, fall to the ground rapidly.

The lanthanides and actinides

The f block contains two periods of elements. The elements in the same period as lanthanum are called lanthanides, and those in the same period as actinium are called actinides.

In this book, you will find out about the lanthanides and actinides and many of their interesting uses.

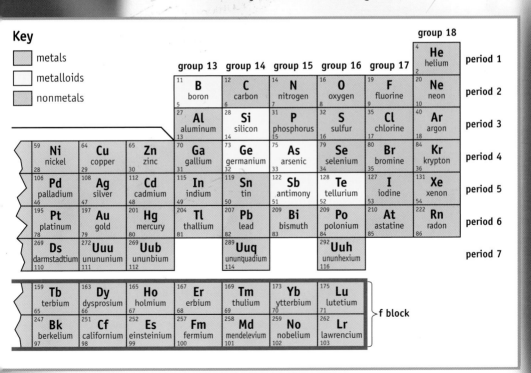

Key

- metals
- metalloids
- nonmetals

group 18

group 13 group 14 group 15 group 16 group 17

| | | | | | | | 4 He helium 2 | period 1 |

| 11 B boron 5 | 12 C carbon 6 | 14 N nitrogen 7 | 16 O oxygen 8 | 19 F fluorine 9 | 20 Ne neon 10 | period 2 |

| 27 Al aluminum 13 | 28 Si silicon 14 | 31 P phosphorus 15 | 32 S sulfur 16 | 35 Cl chlorine 17 | 40 Ar argon 18 | period 3 |

| 59 Ni nickel 28 | 64 Cu copper 29 | 65 Zn zinc 30 | 70 Ga gallium 31 | 73 Ge germanium 32 | 75 As arsenic 33 | 79 Se selenium 34 | 80 Br bromine 35 | 84 Kr krypton 36 | period 4 |

| 106 Pd palladium 46 | 108 Ag silver 47 | 112 Cd cadmium 48 | 115 In indium 49 | 119 Sn tin 50 | 122 Sb antimony 51 | 128 Te tellurium 52 | 127 I iodine 53 | 131 Xe xenon 54 | period 5 |

| 195 Pt platinum 78 | 197 Au gold 79 | 201 Hg mercury 80 | 204 Tl thallium 81 | 207 Pb lead 82 | 209 Bi bismuth 83 | 209 Po polonium 84 | 210 At astatine 85 | 222 Rn radon 86 | period 6 |

| 269 Ds darmstadtium 110 | 272 Uuu unununium 111 | 269 Uub ununbium 112 | | 289 Uuq ununquadium 114 | | 292 Uuh ununhexium 116 | | | period 7 |

f block

| 159 Tb terbium 65 | 163 Dy dysprosium 66 | 165 Ho holmium 67 | 167 Er erbium 68 | 169 Tm thulium 69 | 173 Yb ytterbium 70 | 175 Lu lutetium 71 |

| 247 Bk berkelium 97 | 251 Cf californium 98 | 252 Es einsteinium 99 | 257 Fm fermium 100 | 258 Md mendelevium 101 | 259 No nobelium 102 | 262 Lr lawrencium 103 |

The Lanthanides

All the lanthanides are shiny, silvery metals. They react with water and acids to produce bubbles of hydrogen gas and with oxygen in the air to produce lanthanide oxides. However, there are differences in their reactivity. For example, lanthanum and cerium become covered in a layer of white lanthanum oxide or cerium oxide quite quickly, while lutetium reacts very slowly and can stay shiny for months.

The lanthanides are all solid at room temperature, but some of them are soft enough to cut with a knife, like sodium and the other metals in group 1. The melting points of the lanthanides tend to increase across the period from lanthanum to lutetium and are all much higher than the melting points of the group 1 metals and group 2 metals, such as magnesium. The lanthanides are also much denser than these metals.

Lanthanides	Symbol
Lanthanum	La
Cerium	Ce
Praseodymium	Pr
Neodymium	Nd
Promethium	Pm
Samarium	Sm
Europium	Eu
Gadolinium	Gd
Terbium	Tb
Dysprosium	Dy
Holmium	Ho
Erbium	Er
Thulium	Tm
Ytterbium	Yb
Lutetium	Lu

The lanthanides are a series of fifteen elements in the periodic table, starting with lanthanum and ending with lutetium.

Not so rare

The lanthanides are often called the rare earth metals. Some really are quite rare, such as promethium, which does not seem to exist in the Earth's crust at all! It is found only in very tiny amounts in some uranium ores. On the other hand, cerium is more abundant in the earth's crust than copper.

The lanthanides are used in many things, including lasers, alloys, phosphors, and glass. Most of the lanthanides are found throughout the world in various minerals such as bastnasite, monazite, and xenotime. The main producer of lanthanide ores is China, but the United States, Australia, and India are also major producers. A large deposit of bastnasite, discovered in California in 1949, supplies most of the lanthanides that the United States needs. Bastnasite contains a mixture of different lanthanides in compounds called fluorocarbonates, such as lanthanum fluorocarbonate, $LaCO_3F$. To extract the lanthanide metals from these minerals, they must be processed. Because the lanthanides are so similar to one another, this process is difficult.

▼ *This bar chart shows the amount of each lanthanide in the earth's crust. Copper is a widely used metal that is quite rare; on average there is only 50 grams of copper per metric ton of Earth's crust. In comparison, most of the lanthanides are very rare indeed.*

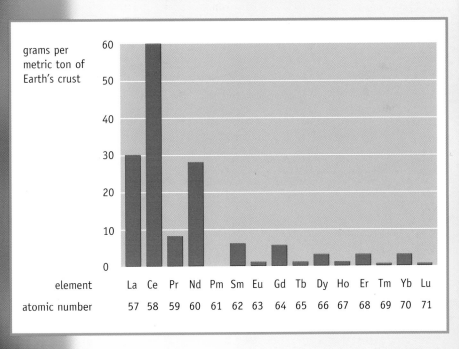

From Ore to Metal

Several complex steps are needed to separate the lanthanides from one another because they are very similar. Also, the minerals in which they are found usually consist of a mixture of lanthanides.

This is monazite, one of the minerals that contains lanthanides. It is also the most important commercial source of thorium, an actinide. ▶

Step 1: Frothy rock

The ore is processed to concentrate the lanthanide minerals and remove unwanted waste materials by a process called froth flotation. The ore is crushed, then ground into a fine powder. Water and special chemicals are mixed with the powdered ore and air is blown through the mixture. The unwanted rock sinks to the bottom while the lanthanide minerals float on the surface in a froth, just like a gritty milkshake!

Step 2: Acid treatment

The concentrated ore is dried and then processed to extract the lanthanides. It is usually treated with hydrochloric acid, which produces lanthanide chlorides, such as lanthanum chloride and lutetium chloride.

Step 3: Solvent extraction

Solvents can dissolve other substances. Water is one of many solvents and is good at dissolving substances, such as salt. Organic solvents, such as turpentine and paint thinner, contain carbon atoms joined to other atoms such as hydrogen and chlorine. These solvents are usually good at dissolving substances like oil and gloss paint. The lanthanide chlorides dissolve a little in kerosene, an organic solvent, when it is mixed with some other chemicals.

Different amounts of each lanthanide chloride can dissolve in this mixture. Lutetium chloride dissolves the most, while lanthanum chloride dissolves the least. The others lie in between. The first time the lanthanide chlorides are dissolved in the kerosene mixture, the kerosene contains more lutetium chloride than lanthanum chloride. If the solvent extraction step is carried out often enough, all the lanthanide chlorides can be separated from one another.

Step 4: Isolate the metals

The metals are isolated from their chlorides by heating them with a reactive metal such as calcium. It is possible to produce very pure metal if this step is repeated enough times, but sometimes the metals are just isolated from the concentrated ore as an alloy (mixture of metals).

The equation for isolating lanthanum is:

lanthanum chloride + calcium $\rightarrow$ lanthanum + calcium chloride

$$2LaCl_3(s) + 3Ca \rightarrow 2La(s) + 3CaCl_2(s)$$

This reaction happens because calcium is more reactive than lanthanum.

Lanthanum, Cerium, and the Twins

139		
La		**lanthanum**
lanthanum		*symbol: La • atomic number: 57 • lanthanide*
57		

What does it look like?   Lanthanum is a silvery metal that is soft enough to cut with a knife. It is one of the most reactive lanthanides, quickly reacting with oxygen in the air to form a layer of lanthanum oxide and bursting into flames when it is heated. It also reacts with water and acids.

Discovery of lanthanum

Lanthanum was discovered in 1839 by the Swedish chemist Carl Mosander. He found the new element in a substance called ceria. This was 36 years after cerium was discovered in the same substance. Mosander named lanthanum after the Greek word meaning "hidden."

What are its main uses?   Lanthanum is mixed with other metals to form a range of useful alloys, including misch metal. This is an alloy containing about 50 percent cerium, 25 percent lanthanum, 18 percent neodymium, and smaller amounts of other lanthanides. It is a pyrophoric alloy, which means that it gives off sparks when it is hit. Misch metal is used in cigarette lighter flints and in the manufacture of hand grenades and tracer bullets. Tracer bullets leave a trail of smoke behind them, so that their path through the air is visible.

Nickel metal hydride batteries, called NiMH for short, are often used in laptop computers, cell phones, video cameras, and cordless tools. They can be recharged quickly and are able to store twice as much energy as a nickel-cadmium (nicad) battery of the same size. The negative electrode in NiMH batteries is made from a nickel-lanthanum alloy, though some designs use misch metal instead of lanthanum. The negative electrode stores large amounts of hydrogen as the battery is being charged and then releases it while the battery is working.

Cracking oil

Crude oil is a mixture of different-sized molecules called hydrocarbons (hydrocarbons contain hydrogen and carbon atoms only). The small hydrocarbons are gases used for fuels, such as propane used in camping grills. The really big ones are used to make asphalt for roads. The medium-sized hydrocarbons are the most useful because they include kerosene, gasoline, and diesel, which are used to power aircraft, cars, and trucks. Crude oil usually contains too many big molecules, but not enough of the medium-sized molecules.

It has to go through a process called cracking at the oil refinery to break down large hydrocarbons into smaller ones, such as gasoline. Catalytic cracking needs catalysts called zeolites. Various lanthanum compounds are usually added to the zeolites to help stabilize them and make them more efficient.

Lanthanum glass

Lanthanum glass contains some lanthanum oxide. It is able to refract, or bend, light better than ordinary glass, so it is used to make high-quality lenses for telescopes and cameras. These lenses are lightweight and produce very good images.

◀ *Cell phones, video cameras, and other portable electronic devices are often powered by nickel metal hydride batteries, which contain a nickel-lanthanum alloy.*

Cerium

140		
Ce	**cerium**	
cerium	symbol: Ce • atomic number: 58 • lanthanide	
58		

What does it look like?   Cerium is one of the most reactive lanthanides, and its chemistry is slightly different from the others. It is a shiny gray metal that reacts with water and acids. It reacts with oxygen in the air to form cerium oxide and bursts into flame when heated.

Discovery of cerium

Cerium was discovered in 1803 by the German chemist Martin Klaproth and at the same time by two Swedish chemists, Wilhlem Hisinger and Jöns Berzelius. The Swedish chemists named the new metal after Ceres, the first (and largest) asteroid to be discovered. Cerium was found in a mineral called ceria. It was eventually shown that ceria contained seven lanthanides in all. Pure cerium was eventually isolated by an American chemist named Alcan Hirsch in 1911.

Where is it found?   Cerium does not exist naturally as an element, but it is quite common in various minerals. There are about 60 grams of cerium in every metric ton of rock in the Earth's crust, making it the most abundant lanthanide. This means it is about as common as lead and much more common than tin. Cerium can be extracted chemically without having to use solvents for complex extraction. To produce the metal from processed lanthanide minerals, cerium chloride is heated with a more reactive metal, such as calcium. About 10,000 metric tons of cerium are produced in the world each year.

What are its main uses?   In a hot car engine, nitrogen and oxygen in the air react together to form nitrogen oxides, which have the chemical formula NOx. If these escape through the exhaust pipe and into the atmosphere, they dissolve in the clouds, causing acid rain. Modern car exhaust systems are fitted with catalytic converters to convert these gases into less harmful ones, such as nitrogen and carbon dioxide. Rhodium is a catalyst that reduces emissions of NOx. The catalyst works better if a little cerium is added to it.

The equation for one of the reactions in a catalytic converter is:

nitrogen oxide + carbon monoxide → nitrogen + carbon dioxide

$$N_2O(g) + CO(g) \rightarrow N_2(g) + CO_2(g)$$

Polystyrene is a plastic that has a huge range of uses, including toys, television sets, and food packaging. To make each molecule of polystyrene, thousands of smaller styrene molecules are joined end to end. The catalyst needed to make the styrene contains cerium carbonate. This helps to keep unwanted chemicals away from the surface of the catalyst, improving its efficiency.

Carbon arc lamps are used for searchlights, movie projectors, and spotlights. When electricity is passed between two electrodes made of graphite and cerium fluoride, a very powerful beam of light is produced.

◀ Searchlights light up the night sky above San Francisco. Powerful lights like these contain electrodes made from graphite and cerium fluoride.

Cerium Oxide

Glass manufacturers use cerium oxide to improve the properties of their glass. Glass naturally has a faint green color because small amounts of iron compounds are trapped in it. If cerium oxide is added during the manufacturing process, it reacts with the iron compounds and removes the green tint. Cerium oxide also prevents the Sun's harmful ultraviolet light from passing through the glass, and it is a particularly important component of aircraft windows. Exposure to ultraviolet radiation is greater the closer you are to the Sun.

Television sets produce small amounts of X rays as part of their normal operation. To prevent them from escaping, barium oxide and strontium oxide are added to the glass. A small amount of cerium oxide is also included to keep the glass from gradually turning brown. Powdered cerium oxide is mixed with water to make a mixture called a slurry. Slurry is used to polish the glass in television sets and mirrors, the surfaces of computer hard disks, and computer chips. Cerium oxide is added to some plastics to keep them from turning brown in sunlight.

▲ Cerium oxide can reduce the amount of harmful ultraviolet light from the Sun that passes through windows into aircraft and cars. Works of art are also protected from ultraviolet light by display cases made with glass containing cerium oxide.

Lanthanides, lasers, and light

The term *laser* stands for *L*ight *A*mplification by *S*timulated *E*mission of *R*adiation. Lasers produce very intense beams of light. The lanthanides are widely used in solid-state lasers, which contain crystals.

A jump and a flash

When energy such as heat or light is supplied to an atom, its electrons can use this extra energy to jump right out of their shell and into a shell farther from the nucleus. These excited electrons cannot stay excited for long and soon drop back to their original shell. When they do this, some atoms give out their extra energy as a flash of light. In a laser, many atoms give out the same type of light at the same time, making an intense beam of laser light.

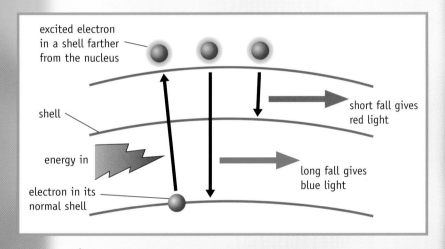

Electrons can jump into another shell if they are given the right amount of energy as heat or light. When they fall back to their normal shell, they give out this energy as light.

A rod-shaped crystal inside the laser contains the atoms that produce the laser beam. To get the laser to work, light is flashed into the crystal from the sides. This excites electrons in the crystal and they produce more light. The two flat ends of the crystal are coated with mirrors, which reflect this light back and forth inside the crystal, so that it becomes more and more intense. Eventually, a flash of laser light comes out of one end of the crystal. Various colors of laser light are produced by including different lanthanides in the crystal.

Praseodymium

141	
Pr	**praseodymium**
praseodymium 59	symbol: Pr • atomic number: 59 • lanthanide

What does it look like?   Praseodymium is a soft, silvery metal that reacts slowly with oxygen in the air, developing a green coating of praseodymium oxide. This flakes off the metal's surface, just as rust flakes off iron. To prevent this, the metal is stored under oil, as is sodium in group 1. Praseodymium reacts with water and acids to produce hydrogen gas and green solutions of praseodymium compounds.

Discovery of praseodymium

In 1839 when Carl Mosander was studying the mineral ceria, he discovered that it contained a metal oxide with a pink color, as well as lanthanum and cerium. Mosander called the oxide didymia, after the Greek word for "twin" because he thought it contained a new metal that was the twin of lanthanum. He called the new metal didymium.

German chemist Carl Auer von Welsbach studied didymia more closely in 1885. He discovered that it contained two metals, not just one, as Mosander had believed. One of the metals produced green compounds, so Auer called it praseodymium, after the Greek words meaning "green twin." The other metal formed pink compounds, and Auer named it neodymium after the Greek words for "new twin.

What are its main uses?   Praseodymium compounds are used to give a yellow color to ceramic tiles and glass. Didymium glass contains didymia, a mixture of praseodymium oxide and neodymium oxide. Glassblowers and welders wear goggles made from this special glass because it filters out light from their equipment that might damage their eyesight.

144	
Nd	
neodymium	
60	

neodymium

symbol: Nd • atomic number: 60 • lanthanide

What does it look like?   A soft, silvery metal, neodymium reacts with oxygen in the air to produce neodymium oxide and is therefore stored under oil. Neodymium reacts with water and acids to produce pale purple solutions of neodymium compounds and hydrogen gas.

What are its main uses?   Neodymium oxide is a sky-blue pigment useful for coloring pottery and glass. It is added to the glass used in television sets and computer monitors because it absorbs yellow light. This helps our eyes tell red and green colors apart. Small amounts of neodymium are often added to the yttrium aluminum garnet (YAG) crystals used in lasers. These neodymium/YAG lasers produce infrared light and are used for welding metals and in medical operations. The small electric motors used in portable CD players and computer disk drives contain permanent magnets made from an alloy composed of neodymium, iron, and boron. This alloy makes a more powerful magnet than iron alone, helping to reduce the size of the electric motor.

▲
Neodymium oxide is a blue pigment added to the glass used in television sets. It absorbs yellow light and so helps our eyes tell the red and green colors apart.

More Members of the Lanthanides

145 Pm promethium 61	**promethium**
	symbol: Pm • atomic number: 61 • lanthanide

What does it look like?   Promethium is very radioactive, and its compounds glow green in the dark. The half-life of its most stable isotope, promethium-145, is less than eighteen years, so promethium is not found naturally in the Earth's crust except in tiny amounts in some uranium ores. Several promethium compounds have been produced but only in small amounts. It really is a rare earth metal!

Discovery of promethium

Jack Marinsky, Lawrence Glendenin, Harold Richter, and Charles Coryell discovered promethium in 1945 in the radioactive waste from a nuclear reactor. Its name comes from the ancient Greek god Prometheus, who was punished by the gods for stealing fire from heaven.

What are its main uses?   Manufacturers need to be sure that plastic film is the right thickness for its purpose, such as wrapping food or packaging goods. Some devices used to measure the thickness of plastic film contain promethium-147. Promethium-147 gives off beta radiation. When this radiation is aimed at the plastic film, the plastic stops some of it. The thicker the plastic, the less radiation gets through to the detector on the other side. Very accurate measurements of the plastic are possible, which can be as thin as 10^{-5} meter (one hundredth of a millimeter).

150 Sm samarium 62	**samarium**
	symbol: Sm • atomic number: 62 • lanthanide

What does it look like?   Samarium is a silvery metal. It reacts slowly with oxygen in the air at room temperature. But when it is heated, samarium catches fire to produce samarium oxide. It reacts with water and acids to produce hydrogen gas and yellow solutions of samarium compounds.

Discovery of samarium

Samarium was discovered in 1879 by a French chemist, Paul-Émile Lecoq. Its name comes from samarskite, the mineral in which it was found. The mineral was originally named after a Russian mine official named Samarski.

What are its main uses? Samarium oxide is added to glass so that it absorbs infrared radiation. When a neodymium laser is in use, some of the infrared laser light can escape from the sides of the crystal, which reduces its efficiency. To prevent this, glass containing samarium oxide is added to the side of the crystal.

The chief use of samarium is in the production of samarium-cobalt alloys for making magnets. These magnets are excellent at keeping their magnetism, even at high temperatures, but they are being replaced by neodymium-iron-boron magnets, which are less expensive. Samarium-cobalt magnets are still used when resistance to high temperatures is important, such as in the aerospace industry.

◀ *This piece of metal is being cut using a laser held by a robot arm. The laser contains an yttrium aluminum garnet (YAG) crystal with small amounts of neodymium. It produces a very powerful laser beam. The glass to the side of the crystal contains samarium oxide to prevent the laser light from escaping.*

Europium

| 152 | **Eu** | **europium** |
| 63 | europium | symbol: Eu • atomic number: 63 • lanthanide |

What does it look like?   Europium, the most reactive lanthanide, is about as reactive as calcium in group 2 and reacts readily with air, water, and acids. Like cerium, europium can be extracted chemically rather than needing complex extraction in solvents. As one of the rarer lanthanides, it is quite expensive.

Discovery of europium

A French chemist, Eugène Demarçay, discovered Europium in some samples of impure samarium in 1896. Demarçay named the new element after Europe, and five years later he managed to isolate a sample of the metal.

What are its main uses?   Europium is mainly used for making phosphors. These are substances that emit light when they are exposed to radiation. Phosphors are very important compounds. Without them you could not see a television picture or the image on a computer monitor.

Most television sets and older computer monitors contain a type of screen called a cathode ray tube (CRT). The image in a CRT is formed when electrons, fired from an electron gun at the back of the CRT, hit the inside of the screen. This is coated with tiny dots containing phosphors, which glow brightly when the electrons hit them. A color picture is made using three different phosphors, each producing red, green, or blue light. The red phosphor is a mixture of europium oxide and yttrium oxide. Phosphors containing europium produce other colors, too, and are important for fluorescent lamps.

Fluorescent lamps

Fluorescent lamps are cheaper to run than ordinary light bulbs because they produce more light and less heat. They are widely used in stores, factories, and schools. They consist of a long glass tube with an electrode at each end.

The tube contains mercury vapor at a very low pressure. When the lamp is switched on, electrons come off the electrodes and cause some of the mercury atoms to become electrically charged mercury ions. Electricity then flows from one end of the lamp to the other through the mercury vapor. This gives some of the mercury atoms extra energy. Electrons in the atoms use this extra energy to jump out of their shells and into shells farther from the nucleus. When these excited electrons drop back to their original shell, they give off light.

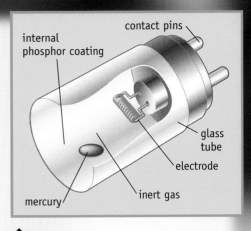

Fluorescent lamps contain mercury vapor at a very low pressure, which gives off invisible ultraviolet light when electricity is passed through it. The inside of the tube is coated with chemicals called phosphors that convert the ultraviolet light into visible light.

Unfortunately, the light given off by mercury atoms is mostly ultraviolet light, which we cannot see. To convert ultraviolet light into visible light, the inside of the fluorescent tube must be coated with phosphors. A mixture of different phosphors is used, each producing a different color. Europium oxide is usually found in phosphors that produce red or blue light. White light is produced when the different phosphors are mixed together in the right amounts.

The fluorescent lamps in these aquaria contain a mixture of different phosphors that produce the desired color of light. Europium is usually found in phosphors that produce red or blue light.

Gadolinium

157 Gd gadolinium 64	**gadolinium** symbol: Gd • atomic number: 64 • lanthanide

What does it look like?   Gadolinium is a silvery metal that gradually turns dull in the air because it reacts with oxygen to form gadolinium oxide. This flakes off the surface of the metal, as rust flakes off iron. It also reacts with water and acids.

Discovery of gadolinium

The Swiss chemist Jean de Marignac discovered gadolinium in 1880. He found it in a mineral called gadolinite, which was named in honor of the Finnish chemist Johan Gadolin.

What are its main uses?   Gadolinium has a very high magnetic moment, which means that it is highly responsive to magnetic fields. It is useful in technologies such as magnetic resonance imaging and is used in medicine, magneto-optical data recording, and computing.

Magnetic resonance imaging, or MRI for short, allows doctors to examine the insides of their patients without opening them up. The patient lies inside a large, ring-shaped magnet, and harmless radio waves are passed through the patient's body, causing some of its atoms to give off signals. The signals are detected by the machine, and a computer creates an image of the patient's insides. To produce a clearer image, compounds containing gadolinium can be injected into the patient's bloodstream before MRI.

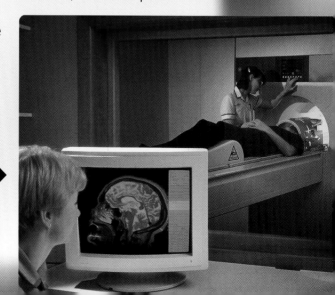

A magnetic resonance imaging (MRI) scanner is being used to scan the brain of a patient.

| 159 |
| Tb |
| terbium |
| 65 |

terbium

symbol: Tb • atomic number: 65 • lanthanide

What does it look like? Terbium is a silvery metal that is soft enough to cut with a knife, like sodium and potassium in group 1. It reacts slowly with oxygen in the air to form terbium oxide and also reacts with water and acids.

Discovery and isolation of terbium

Carl Mosander discovered terbium in gadolinite in 1843, the year after he discovered erbium. The new element was named terbium because the gadolinite was found near the village of Ytterby, near Stockholm.

What are its main uses? Terbium compounds are used in phosphors that produce green light. These phosphors are used in fluorescent lamps with the europium phosphors. The green color in television pictures is provided by phosphors made from gadolinium compounds with small amounts of terbium.

Terbium-gadolinium alloys are used for a type of rewritable computer disk called a magneto-optical (MO) disk. An MO disk looks like an ordinary CD, but data can be recorded on it and then easily erased.

▲
This digital camcorder can record 11,000 photographs, or more than two hours of video, on a magneto-optical disk that contains a layer of terbium-gadolinium alloy.

Dysprosium

163 **Dy** dysprosium 66	**dysprosium** *symbol: Dy • atomic number: 66 • lanthanide*

What does it look like?   Dysprosium is a silvery metal that can be cut with a knife. It reacts slowly with oxygen in the air to form dysprosium oxide. It also reacts with water and acids.

Discovery of dysprosium

Paul-Émile Lecoq, the French chemist who discovered samarium in 1879, discovered dysprosium seven years later. However, he was unable to isolate the metal itself, hence its name, which is from the Greek words meaning "hard to get."

What are its main uses?   Dysprosium oxide is added to the special ceramics used to make capacitors. These are devices that can store electric charge and are widely used in electronic circuits. Nuclear reactors naturally produce high-speed neutrons, but some of these must be absorbed to control the nuclear reaction. Otherwise, there would be a nuclear explosion. Dysprosium oxide is one of the substances used in the control rods for some nuclear reactors because it has a high melting point and is very good at absorbing neutrons.

A type of lamp called a medium source rare earth lamp, or MSR lamp for short, contains dysprosium and holmium compounds mixed with other compounds. MSR lamps produce light with a good balance of color. They are often used to light movie sets and theater stages, so scenes look natural rather than strangely colored.

Holmium:YAG lasers produce a beam of invisible infrared light. Surgeons use these lasers to repair damaged joints. ▶

165	
Ho	
holmium	
67	

holmium

symbol: Ho • atomic number: 67 • lanthanide

What does it look like?　Holmium reacts slowly with oxygen in damp air to produce holmium oxide, but it does not react in dry air. It reacts with water and acids and, like most lanthanides, is a soft, silvery metal.

Discovery of holmium

Two Swiss chemists, Jacques-Louis Soret and Marc Delafontaine, discovered holmium in 1878, and Swedish chemist Per Teodor Cleve extracted it a year later. Cleve named the element after the Latin name for Stockholm—Holmia.

What are its main uses?　Holmium is used in surgical lasers called holmium:YAG lasers. These are solid-state lasers containing a crystal of yttrium aluminum garnet (the YAG in their name). Small amounts of different lanthanides can be added to YAG crystals (called doping) to produce different colors of laser light. The crystals in holmium:YAG lasers are doped with small amounts of holmium and produce short pulses of invisible infrared light, which can briefly heat up a target. Surgeons use holmium:YAG lasers to repair damaged

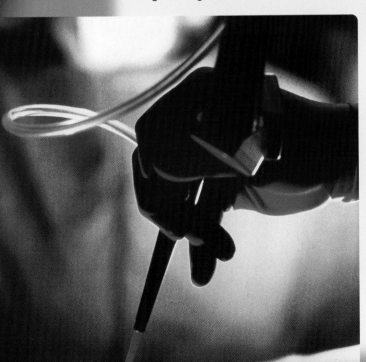

knees and other joints and to break up painful kidney stones. Eye surgeons use these lasers to alter the shape of the front of the eye very slightly, improving the vision of people with farsightedness. These people cannot focus properly on objects close to them and usually need glasses or contact lenses.

Erbium

167 Er erbium 68	**erbium** *symbol: Er • atomic number: 68 • anthanide*

What does it look like?   Erbium is a soft, silvery metal. It reacts with water and acids, but slowly with oxygen in the air.

Discovery of erbium

Carl Mosander discovered erbium in gadolinite in 1842. The new element was named after Ytterby, Sweden, where gadolinite was found. Pure erbium was first isolated in 1934.

What are its main uses?   A small amount of erbium is mixed with vanadium, a hard metal that is often alloyed with steel to make it softer and more workable. Erbium oxide is a pleasant pink color and is used to color ceramics and glass.

Erbium is useful in amplifiers for fiber optic cables, which carry telephone and computer signals over long distances. Signals are sent as light through thin glass fibers, but as the light travels, it begins to fade. If it fades too much, the signal is lost so amplifiers are needed at intervals along the cable. Erbium-doped fiber amplifiers boost the signal using laser light. They work well because

the light released by the erbium exactly matches the color of the light used in the signal.

Erbium:YAG lasers are particularly useful for cosmetic surgery, such as smoothing skin and removing wrinkles. They produce pulses of infrared light that go only a tenth of a millimeter into the skin, removing just the outer layer.

169 **Tm** thulium 69	**Thulium** *symbol: Tm • atomic number: 69 • lanthanide*

What does it look like? Thulium is a silvery metal that is soft enough to be cut with a knife, like sodium in group 1. It reacts with oxygen in the air to form thulium oxide and reacts easily with water and acids.

Discovery of thulium
Thulium was discovered in a sample of impure erbium oxide by the Swedish chemist Per Teodor Cleve in 1879. He named the new element after Thule, the Greek name for Scandinavia.

What are its main uses? Thulium metal is very expensive. It only became available in the late 1900s and has few uses. Natural samples of thulium contain only one isotope, thulium-169, which is not radioactive. However, if it is exposed to neutron radiation, it is converted into radioactive thulium-170, which gives off low-energy gamma rays. These are similar to X rays, so thulium-170 is used in portable X-ray machines by engineers checking machines for damage, similar to the way doctors check their patients for broken bones using X rays.

◀ *Fiber optic cables like these carry telephone and computer signals over long distances. Erbium is used in amplifiers that boost the signal as it travels along the cable.*

Ytterbium

173 **Yb** ytterbium 70	**ytterbium** *symbol: Yb • atomic number: 70 • lanthanide*

What does it look like?   Ytterbium (pronounced it-ur-bee-um) is a soft, silvery metal that reacts with water and acids and slowly with oxygen in the air.

Discovery of ytterbium

Swiss chemist Jean de Marignac discovered ytterbium in gadolinite in 1878. Other scientists found the element later and called it alderbarania and neoytterbia. Chemists finally agreed to name it ytterbium after Ytterby, Sweden, where gadolinite was found.

What are its main uses?   When traffic crosses a bridge, the weight of the vehicles exerts a force on the bridge and puts it under stress. One way to measure the stress is to use a device called a stress gauge. This is a small handheld device that can accurately measure stresses in rocks, buildings, and bridges. One type of gauge monitors ytterbium to detect the stresses. Ytterbium conducts electricity, like all metals, but when it is pulled its resistance increases. This means that it becomes more difficult for electricity to flow through. If an object is put under stress, the ytterbium is pulled slightly and its resistance increases. This change in resistance can be detected using an electronic circuit, showing how much stress is acting on the object.

This road has been damaged by an earthquake. ▶
You can see how far the road has been moved by the yellow lines each side of the large crack. Stress gauges containing ytterbium can measure the forces in rocks, buildings and bridges that lead to this sort of damage.

175	
Lu	**lutetium**
lutetium	*symbol: Lu • atomic number: 71 • lanthanide*
71	

What does it look like?   Lutetium (pronounced loo-tee-shum) is the hardest and most dense lanthanide. It is a silvery metal that reacts slowly with air, water, and acids.

Discovery of lutetium

Lutetium was found in gadolinite, as was ytterbium. Carl Auer von Welsbach, a German chemist, discovered lutetium in 1907 and called it cassiopeium. A French chemist named Georges Urbain also discovered it in the same year and named it after Lutetia Parisiorum, the Roman name for Paris.

What are its main uses?   Crystals of lutetium compounds, containing small amounts of cerium, are used in medical imaging devices. These crystals give off a flash of light when exposed to radiation and are used in positron emission tomography, known as PET for short. Doctors can use PET to help them diagnose problems with the brain, such as clots and damage from strokes. The patient is injected with a harmless amount of a radioactive substance that gives off subatomic particles called positrons. These are similar to electrons but have a positive electrical charge instead of a negative charge. The PET scanner detects these positrons and creates an image of the patient's brain.

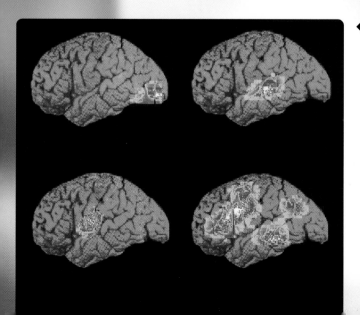

◀ *Crystals containing lutetium and cerium are used in positron emission tomography (PET), which allows doctors to creates images of the brain. These PET scans show how different areas of the brain become particularly active when we see, hear, or speak.*

The Actinides and Radioactivity

Four of the actinides occur naturally: actinium, thorium, protactinium, and uranium. The other eleven actinides, including plutonium, are all made by nuclear reactions. All the actinides are silvery metals that are solid at room temperature, and they are all radioactive. Many of them are found or made in tiny amounts and most of their uses depend on their radioactive properties. There are different forms of each actinide, called isotopes, which can produce different types of radiation.

The actinides are a series of fifteen elements in the periodic table, starting with actinium and ending with lawrencium. ▶

Actinides	Symbol
Actinium	Ac
Thorium	Th
Protactinium	Pa
Uranium	U
Neptunium	Np
Plutonium	Pu
Americium	Am
Curium	Cm
Berkelium	Bk
Californium	Cf
Einsteinium	Es
Fermium	Fm
Mendelevium	Md
Nobelium	No
Lawrencium	Lr

Isotopes

Atoms of an element always have the same number of protons in their nucleus. Uranium atoms, for example, always have 92 protons, but the number of neutrons can vary.

Isotopes are atoms of an element that have the same number of protons and electrons but different numbers of neutrons. The most common isotope of uranium is uranium-238. The nucleus of a uranium-238 atom has 92 protons and 146 neutrons. There are several other isotopes of uranium, including uranium-235, which has only 143 neutrons. Uranium-235 behaves chemically just like uranium-238 because it still has 92 protons in its nucleus.

Half-life

The nucleus of some atoms can break up, or decay, into smaller pieces. Nobody can predict when an individual atom will decay, but if we study huge numbers of atoms we can say how long it takes for half of them to decay. The time it takes for half the atoms in an isotope to decay is called its half-life. This time cannot be changed by heating and cooling or by any chemical reactions.

Some isotopes have very unstable nuclei and they decay very quickly. The half-life of uranium-231, for example, is just over four days. Other isotopes are much more stable, like uranium-238, which has a half-life of around 4.5 billion years.

Radiation

When a nucleus of an unstable element decays, it can become an isotope of a different element or another isotope of the same element. Radiation, given out when an isotope decays, can pass through either the air, our bodies, plastic, or metal, depending on which type of radiation is. Gamma radiation is the most penetrating type; alpha radiation is the least penetrating; in between is a third type of radiation called beta radiation.

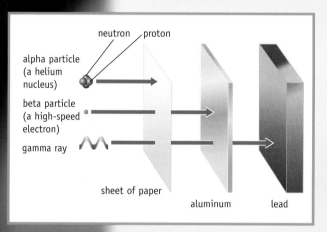

Alpha radiation is easily blocked by paper. Beta radiation can pass through paper but is blocked by sheets of aluminum. Gamma radiation passes through paper and aluminum, but is blocked by thick sheets of lead.

Radiation hazards and health

If radiation passes into our bodies, it can damage the chemicals in our cells, particularly a complex long-chain molecule called deoxyribonucleic acid (DNA). DNA is the molecule that contains our genetic code. This is the code used by our cells to make the different proteins they need. If part of a DNA molecule is damaged by radiation, the code gets scrambled and may produce a protein that does not work properly. Some damaged proteins can make the cell divide uncontrollably to make many new cells, causing cancer. However, radiation used in a controlled way can help cure cancer. If a cancer cell is given a very high dose of radiation, its DNA becomes so damaged that it dies. Treating cancer using radiation is called radiotherapy.

This hazard symbol is used to warn people that the chemical inside the container is radioactive.

Actinium

227		actinium
Ac		symbol: Ac • atomic number: 89 • actinide
actinium		
89		

What does it look like?   Actinium is a soft, silvery metal that reacts with air and water. It is intensely radioactive, which is why it glows blue in the dark. It is difficult to study actinium's chemistry because it is so rare, but it seems to be very similar to lanthanum, which is immediately above it in the periodic table.

Discovery of actinium

The French chemist André Debierne discovered actinium in 1899 while helping Marie and Pierre Curie in their research. The Curies made many important discoveries involving radioactive elements and radiation. In 1898, they discovered two new elements, radium and polonium, in a uranium ore called pitchblende. Debierne discovered actinium in the huge amount of waste material from this research and named it after the Greek word for "ray."

What are its main uses?   A metric ton of pitchblende contains only about 0.1 microgram of actinium, but it can be made artificially in a nuclear reactor by exposing radium to neutron radiation. Actinium has not been used to make anything because it is so rare, and only a few actinium compounds have ever been made. It is useful only for the intense radiation it produces and is used mostly for scientific research.

A sample of actinium oxide in a radiation-resistant quartz container. ▶

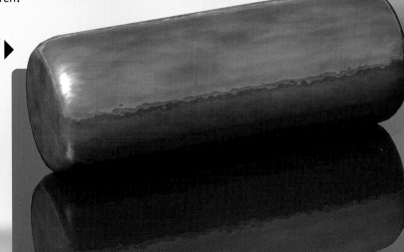

Radioactive decay series

Unstable elements give off radiation and change into other elements until a stable element is formed.

Actinium-227 decays to form lead-207, a stable isotope that is not radioactive. However, actinium itself results from the decay of uranium-235. Actinium is found in tiny amounts in uranium ores such as pitchblende because some of the uranium-235 atoms have decayed. Scientists have discovered many other nuclear reactions like this one and have pieced them together like jigsaws to form decay series.

The actinium decay series

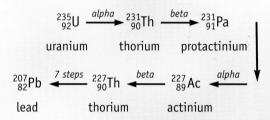

The other elements in the series, thorium, protactinium, and uranium, are the three other naturally occurring actinides.

Chemical symbols

The full chemical symbol for uranium-238 is $^{238}_{92}U$. The bottom number is called the atomic number, which indicates the number of protons in the nucleus. The top number is called the mass number, and it shows the number of protons added to the number of neutrons. If you want to figure out how many neutrons there are in the nucleus, you just subtract the bottom number from the top number. So the number of neutrons in an atom of $^{238}_{92}U$ is 238 minus 92, which equals 146.

Thorium

232 Th thorium 90	**thorium** symbol: Th • atomic number: 90 • actinide

What does it look like?   Thorium is a soft, silvery metal that reacts slowly with water and hydrochloric acid. It gradually becomes covered by a layer of black thorium oxide as it reacts with oxygen in the air. However, it burns with a bright white light if it is heated in air.

Discovery and extraction of thorium

The Swedish chemist Jöns Berzelius discovered thorium in 1828 in a mineral called thorite (thorium silicate). He named it after Thor, the Norse god of thunder and war. Thorium is also found in other minerals, such as thorianite (thorium oxide). However, monazite (one of the lanthanide minerals) is the most important commercial source of thorium. Large deposits of thorium are found in Australia, India, Norway, and the United States, and about 30,000 metric tons of thorium are extracted each year. Heating thorium oxide with a reactive metal such as calcium produces thorium metal.

What are its main uses?   Thorium oxide is a solid with the highest melting point of all the oxides (nearly 3,300 °C, or 5,972 °F). It is widely used where resistance to high temperatures is important, such as in laboratory crucibles. Tungsten-thorium alloys, containing 2 percent thorium oxide, are used in tungsten inert gas welding, or TIG for short.

Electrodes made from tungsten-thorium alloys are used in tungsten inert gas welding, shown here. ▶

In TIG, heat is generated by making electricity arc, or jump, between two tungsten-thorium alloy electrodes. The small amount of thorium in the electrodes makes them harder, and it is easier to start the electric arc. Magnesium-thorium alloys that contain 3 percent thorium are used to make the skin panels and nose cones of missiles.

Thorium oxide is used in gas mantles for camping lanterns. Carl Auer Von Welsbach, the German chemist who discovered neodymium, praseodymium, and lutetium, invented the Welsbach gas mantle in 1885. He soaked cotton wicks in solutions of lanthanum nitrate, cerium nitrate, or thorium nitrate, left them to dry, and then burned them. Welsbach found the remains formed a mesh of metal oxide, which when heated in a flame, emitted bright, white light. He discovered that thorium oxide with 1 percent cerium oxide made the best mantles. Welsbach gas mantles were widely used for lighting streets and homes until the mid-1900s, when gas lighting was eventually replaced by electric lighting.

Since Polish-born chemist Marie Curie showed that thorium is radioactive in 1898, it has mostly been replaced by other metals, especially the lanthanides, but it is used as an ingredient in some nuclear fuels.

The thorium decay series

Thorium decays to form stable lead-208, which is not radioactive. There is a thorium decay series, which is slightly different from the actinium decay series, although actinium is still produced. Radium, a group 2 element discovered by Marie Curie in 1898, is also formed.

The thorium decay series

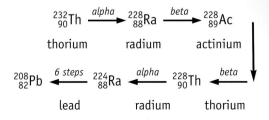

$$^{232}_{90}\text{Th} \xrightarrow{alpha} {}^{228}_{88}\text{Ra} \xrightarrow{beta} {}^{228}_{89}\text{Ac}$$

thorium   radium   actinium

$$^{208}_{82}\text{Pb} \xleftarrow{6 \ steps} {}^{224}_{88}\text{Ra} \xleftarrow{alpha} {}^{228}_{90}\text{Th} \xleftarrow{beta}$$

lead   radium   thorium

231	protactinium
Pa	symbol: Pa • atomic number: 91 • actinide
protactinium	
91	

What does it look like?   Protactinium is the third rarest natural element, which makes it very expensive. It is very radioactive and needs to be handled with great care. Little is known about protactinium's other chemical properties. It has no uses apart from scientific research.

Discovery of protactinium

When Dimitri Mendeleev developed his periodic table in the late 1800s, he left some gaps for elements he believed were yet to be discovered. He left one gap between thorium (atomic number 90) and uranium (atomic number 92). With the help of the periodic table, chemists predicted the properties of the missing element, which made it easier to search for. In 1913, Kasimir Fajans and Otto Göhring managed to find an isotope of the missing element while studying the uranium decay series. They had discovered protactinium-234. They called it brevium because it has such a brief half-life—just over six hours!

In 1917, two groups of scientists discovered another protactinium isotope in pitchblende. One of the groups, Otto Hahn and Lise Meitner, suggested the name protoactinium because the element decayed to form actinium. The name was shortened to protactinium in 1949. Working in the United States in 1927, Aristid Grosse isolated a tiny amount of white protactinium oxide. Seven years later he managed to produce some pure protactinium by converting the oxide into protactinium iodide. When he heated this, it broke down to form protactinium and iodine.

The uranium decay series

Protactinium was discovered while scientists were studying the decay series of uranium. The most common natural uranium isotope, uranium-238, slowly decays to form thorium-234. Thorium-234 gives off beta radiation and becomes protactinium-234, which in turn eventually decays to form lead-206. Lead-206 is a stable isotope and not radioactive.

The uranium decay series

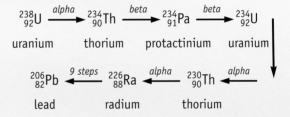

$$^{238}_{92}U \xrightarrow{alpha} {}^{234}_{90}Th \xrightarrow{beta} {}^{234}_{91}Pa \xrightarrow{beta} {}^{234}_{92}U$$

uranium   thorium   protactinium   uranium

$$^{206}_{82}Pb \xleftarrow{9\ steps} {}^{226}_{88}Ra \xleftarrow{alpha} {}^{230}_{90}Th \xleftarrow{alpha}$$

lead   radium   thorium

*Protactinium results from the decay of uranium, which is why it is found in uranium **ores**.*

The four naturally occurring actinides

The four naturally occurring actinides are closely related through the various radioactive decay series. This explains why actinium, thorium, and protactinium are found in uranium ores and why some are rare while others are not. Uranium is the last naturally occurring element. It is relatively abundant and has many uses.

◄ *Otto Hahn (1879–1968) and Lise Meitner (1878–1968) discovered an isotope of protactinium in 1917. They named the new element protoactinium, which was shortened to protactinium in 1949.*

Uranium

238 **U** uranium 92	**uranium** *symbol: U • atomic number: 92 • actinide*

What does it look like?
Uranium is a silvery metal that is nearly as dense as gold. Although it reacts with acids, it reacts slowly with oxygen in the air unless it is powdered. Then it bursts into flames. It is radioactive and produces alpha radiation.

This is a disk of uranium metal. The gloves protect the person's hands from the radiation that uranium emits. ▶

Discovery of uranium

Martin Klaproth, a German chemist, discovered uranium in 1789. He found it in the mineral pitchblende, which contains uranium dioxide. Klaproth named the new element after the planet Uranus, which had been discovered by William Herschel eight years earlier. In 1841, French chemist Eugène Péligot became the first chemist to isolate uranium metal, by heating uranium tetrachloride with potassium.

Where is it found? Uranium is not found as a pure metal, but it is fairly abundant in various minerals. On average, there are about 2 grams (0.07 ounce)of uranium in every metric ton of rock in the earth's crust. It about as common as tin and more plentiful than gold or silver. The most important uranium ore is pitchblende, also called uraninite. The largest deposits of uranium ore are found in Australia, Kazakhstan, and Canada. About 40,000 tons of uranium are produced in the world each year, mostly in Canada.

Yellow cake

Several complex steps are needed to extract uranium from its ore. The ores are processed to produce the solid sodium diuranate, $Na_2U_2O_7$, which is called yellow cake. This is the form in which uranium is usually bought and sold.

Isolating uranium metal

Uranium metal is isolated from yellow cake in two main steps. The yellow cake is first processed to produce uranium dioxide, UO_2. This is heated with hydrogen fluoride to produce uranium tetrafluoride, UF_4.

The equation for a step in uranium ore refining is:

uranium dioxide + hydrogen fluoride → uranium tetrafluoride + water

$$UO_2(s) + 4HF(g) \rightarrow UF_4(g) + 2H_2O(l)$$

This is a reaction between a base (uranium dioxide) and an acid (hydrogen fluoride) to produce a salt and water.

Uranium metal is produced from uranium tetrafluoride using the Ames process, which is similar to Péligot's original method. The uranium tetrafluoride is heated to over 1000 °C with a reactive metal such as magnesium, producing uranium metal and waste containing magnesium fluoride.

The equation for the Ames Process is:

uranium tetrafluoride + magnesium → uranium + magnesium fluoride

$$UF_4(s) + 2Mg(s) \rightarrow U(s) + 2MgF_2(s)$$

Uranium and the discovery of radioactivity

Henri Becquerel discovered radioactivity by accident in 1896. He left photographic plates next to uranium ore in the dark. When he developed them they were foggy. The radiation from the uranium had caused the chemicals in the photographic plate to break down, just as they do when light hits them.

Uses of uranium

Uranium is used as a fuel in nuclear power plants and in the manufacture of nuclear weapons. Natural uranium is a mixture of different uranium isotopes, though less than 1 percent is uranium-235. However, nuclear power plants need enriched uranium containing 3 percent to 5 percent uranium-235, and atomic weapons require highly enriched uranium containing over 90 percent uranium-235. Natural uranium has to be processed to increase the amount of uranium-235. The leftover material is called depleted uranium because it contains a third of the uranium-235 found in natural uranium. Depleted uranium is less radioactive than natural uranium because it contains less uranium-235.

Depleted uranium

Uranium is a hard and very dense metal, almost as dense as gold or tungsten. Depleted uranium is therefore useful for making objects that need to be small and heavy, such as the armor-piercing shells used by the military to destroy tanks. It is also made into sinker bars, which are used by the oil industry to sink scientific instruments to the bottom of oil wells.

In the past, depleted uranium was used in aircraft as a counterweight to maintain the center of gravity. Jumbo jets built in the 1960s each contained about 350 kilograms of depleted uranium in their tail sections. This has now been replaced by tungsten because of the dangers of radiation. Depleted uranium is also used to prepare uranium compounds for other uses.

Electron microscopy

The electron microscope allows biologists to study objects that are too small to be seen with an ordinary light microscope. They add a drop of uranium acetate (usually known as uranyl acetate) solution to stain their samples. This helps to give a good image in the microscope because uranium is very dense and scatters electrons well.

Glazes and glass

Uranium compounds are colored and make good pigments. Although they were used in glass and pottery glazes for many years, modern glass and glazes do not contain uranium compounds because of the radiation they produce. Vaseline glass is a type of antique glass that was widely used to produce ornamental objects. It contains uranium(VI) oxide and has an attractive greenish-yellow appearance. Glass containing a small amount of uranium(IV) oxide is yellow with a green tint, while uranium(V) oxide makes glass with a black tint. Pottery glazes containing sodium diuranate, $Na_2U_2O_7$, are yellow, while uranium oxide, U_3O_8, produces an olive-green glaze. Glazes containing uranium(IV) oxide are bright red-yellow.

▲
These attractive pieces of glassware are made from greenish-yellow Vaseline glass, which is a type of antique glass that contains uranium(VI) oxide.

Roman numbers

Chemists use Roman numerals to tell the different uranium oxides apart. The Roman numeral indicates the positive charge on the uranium. Uranium dioxide, UO_2, is uranium (IV) oxide (uranium four oxide). Uranium(V) oxide (uranium five oxide) is U_2O_5, and UO_3 is uranium(VI) oxide (uranium six oxide).

The most important uses of uranium, however, involve harnessing its nuclear properties.

Bombs and Reactors

When an atom is split, the process is called fission; heat and radiation are produced. This may happen suddenly if the nucleus is unstable. In this case it is called spontaneous fission. Some atoms can be forced to split by firing neutrons at them. This is called induced fission and is the process behind atomic bomb and nuclear reactor technology.

Chain reactions

Uranium-235 is particularly easy to split by induced fission. When a neutron hits the nucleus of a uranium-235 atom, the nucleus becomes unstable and splits into two smaller ones. Heat and gamma radiation are released and three more neutrons are shot out. These neutrons may go on to split more uranium-235 atoms. This is called a chain reaction.

Critical mass

In a piece of uranium where induced fission is happening, some of the neutrons escape without splitting other uranium atoms. If the piece of uranium is too small, most of the neutrons escape and the chain reaction eventually stops. If there is the right amount of uranium, called the critical mass, the chain reaction continues at a steady rate (on average each uranium atom split causes one more atom to split). However, if there is too much uranium, called a supercritical mass, something else happens.

Atomic bombs

In a supercritical mass, each uranium atom split causes more than one other atom to split, causing a runaway nuclear reaction. So much energy is released in a short time that a nuclear explosion happens. A typical bomb contains a supercritical mass of uranium, but in separate pieces to stop the nuclear reaction from starting. When these pieces are slammed together to make a single ball, the bomb detonates, or explodes. The first atomic bomb used in a war was a uranium bomb called Little Boy. It exploded over the Japanese city of Hiroshima on August 6, 1945. About 66,000 people were killed and 69,000 were injured directly. Many people died of cancer long after the bombing.

Nuclear reactors

The first nuclear reactor was built by a team led by Enrico Fermi at the University of Chicago and was started up on December 2, 1942. The reaction in a nuclear reactor is controlled so that it is critical or just slightly supercritical. This is achieved by using boron control rods. These absorb neutrons and keep them from splitting uranium atoms.

The heat produced by the nuclear reaction is used to make steam. This drives turbines that turn electricity generators, just as in a conventional coal-fired power plant. Nuclear power plants provide factories and millions of homes with electricity.

◀ *This is a nuclear reactor core viewed from above. In the middle of the photograph you can see a used fuel rod being removed from the reactor under water.*

When things go wrong

Nuclear power plants are designed to be very safe because if things go wrong the consequences are disastrous. In 1979, at the Three Mile Island nuclear power plant in Pennsylvania, part of the reactor core was not cooled properly. The reactor was contaminated and small amounts of radioactive substances escaped, but there were no immediate deaths or injuries.

Seven years later, a nuclear reactor exploded near Chernobyl in the Ukraine. It was not a nuclear explosion, but huge amounts of radioactive substances still escaped into the atmosphere and were spread by the winds and air currents throughout Europe and beyond. Local people still suffer from illnesses because of their exposure to radiation.

CHAPTER 7

The Artificial Actinides

Uranium atoms are the heaviest natural atoms, with 92 protons in the nucleus. Atoms with more protons, called transuranium elements, have to be made artificially by converting one element into another. It is not possible to do this using a chemical reaction. The only way one element can be converted into another is by a nuclear reaction. Whenever a nuclear bomb explodes, some transuranium elements are made. Einsteinium and fermium were discovered in the fallout from the first hydrogen bomb.

What's in a bomb?

There are two basic types of nuclear reactions, and both produce radiation and a lot of energy. Fission reactions happen when the nuclei of large atoms, such as uranium and plutonium, break apart. Fusion reactions occur when the nuclei of atoms, which can be small ones, such as hydrogen, join together to make larger nuclei. Atomic bombs use fission reactions, and hydrogen bombs use fusion reactions.

The nuclear reactions in nuclear reactors also make some transuranium elements. Americium, the fourth transuranium element discovered, was found in the waste from a nuclear reactor. The rest of the artificial actinides were made by smashing high-speed particles into metal targets using a machine called a cyclotron.

The cyclotron is a type of particle accelerator invented by Ernest Lawrence, a physicist at the University of California at Berkeley. Lawrence won a Nobel prize for his invention. A particle accelerator makes particles move faster and faster. In a cyclotron, the particles are shot around and around in a spiral. The first cyclotron was built in 1931 and was only about 10 centimeters (4 inches) in diameter. Modern cyclotrons can be many meters in diameter and accelerate particles to about 75 percent of the speed of light. If you could hitch a ride on one of those particles, you could get to the Sun in 11 minutes! For a cyclotron to work, the particles must have an electrical charge. They are usually positively charged ions (atoms with electrons removed).

▲
This scientist is working on a small cyclotron, a type of particle accelerator that whirls subatomic particles around at high speeds.

| 237 Np neptunium 93 | **neptunium** *symbol: Np • atomic number: 93 • actinide* |

What does it look like? Neptunium was the first transuranium element to be discovered. It is a silvery metal, a solid at room temperature and, like all the other transuranium elements, radioactive. It reacts with oxygen to form brown neptunium oxide and reacts with water and acids. Solutions of neptunium compounds have a violet color.

Discovery of neptunium

In 1940 Edwin McMillan and Philip Abelson bombarded some uranium-238 with neutrons at the Lawrence Berkeley National Laboratory, in California, and made a new element. The new element was called neptunium because it is the next element after uranium in the periodic table and Neptune is the next planet from the Sun after Uranus. Neptunium is made in nuclear reactors as part of their normal operation and is now extracted from nuclear wastes. However, it has little practical use apart from scientific research.

Plutonium

244 Pu plutonium 94	**plutonium**
	symbol: Pu • atomic number: 94 • actinide

What does it look like?   Plutonium is solid at room temperature. It is a silvery metal that reacts with oxygen in the air, forming a layer of plutonium oxide on its surface that gives it a faint yellow color. Plutonium feels warm because the alpha radiation it produces releases energy. It reacts with water and acids.

Discovery of plutonium

Plutonium was discovered by Glenn Seaborg, Edwin McMillan, Joseph Kennedy, and Arthur Wahl in 1940. They used a cyclotron at the Lawrence Berkeley National Laboratory to bombard uranium atoms with deuterons. Deuterons are ions of a hydrogen isotope and consist of a proton and neutron stuck together. Plutonium was the second transuranium element discovered, and it was named after Pluto, the next planet from the Sun after Neptune.

What are its main uses?   All nuclear reactors produce plutonium-239 from uranium-238 as part of their normal operation. The spent fuel is processed to extract the plutonium-239, which is then used as a fuel itself in a type of nuclear reactor called a fast-breeder reactor. Plutonium-239 is also used in nuclear weapons because its critical mass is about one-fifth of the critical mass of uranium-235. This means that weapons designers can produce smaller bombs or more powerful bombs of a similar size.

The second and last nuclear bomb used in World War II was a plutonium bomb called Fat Man. It was dropped on Nagasaki, Japan, on August 9, 1945. This bomb killed about 39,000 people and injured 25,000, not including the additional deaths caused by cancer long after the bombing.

Radioisotope thermoelectric generators

Plutonium-238 is used in radioisotope thermoelectric generators. These are called RTGs for short and are nuclear batteries. In an RTG, heat is produced by the radioactive decay of plutonium-238, which warms a device called a thermocouple. This consists of two different metals joined together and produces electricity when heated.

RTGs are very reliable because they have no moving parts and their small size makes them ideal for powering space probes. The RTGs in modern probes are all powered by plutonium-238 because its half-life is nearly 88 years, allowing space probes to remain working in space for a long time. Other radioactive isotopes, such as polonium-210, have been tried, but their shorter half-lives cause probes to run out of power too quickly.

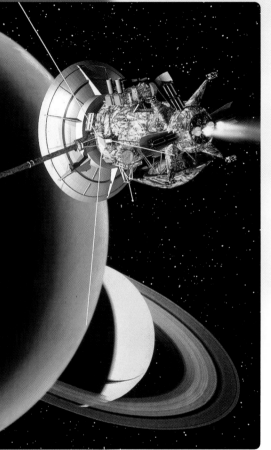

◀ The Cassini-Huygens *space probe, launched in October 1997, was designed to reach Saturn after a seven-year journey. Electricity for the probe is generated using three RTGs (radioisotope thermoelectric generators) that contain plutonium-238.*

Not in my backyard!

The plutonium-239 produced in nuclear reactors has a very long half-life of 24,110 years. The disposal of this radioactive material is a huge problem. It cannot be left in the reactor or dumped into an ordinary garbage bin and must be prevented from falling into the hands of terrorists, who might use it to make a bomb. Many countries are trying to find places where they can bury it deep underground, but scientists have to predict whether it will still be safe in the future, which is a hard thing to do. Not surprisingly, nobody wants to live near a nuclear storage site.

Americium

243 Am americium 95	**americium** *symbol: Am • atomic number: 95 • actinide*

What does it look like?   Americium is a dense, silvery metal, which is solid at room temperature, but easily shaped. Americium reacts with oxygen in the air to make americium oxide and also reacts with water and acids. Several americium compounds have been made, including brown americium oxide and pink americium chloride. Americium needs careful handling because it gives off alpha and gamma radiation.

Discovery of americium

Americium was the fourth transuranium element to be discovered. Glenn Seaborg, Ralph James, Leon Morgan, and Albert Ghiorso, working at the University of Chicago in 1944, found it in a sample of plutonium from a nuclear reactor. The new element was named after the United States of America, where it was found.

Americium is used in smoke detectors. When a house fire like this one breaks out, smoke detectors save lives by giving an early warning so the residents can escape in time.

What are its main uses? The uses of americium rely on the radiation it produces. Engineers find its gamma rays useful for checking machines for cracks and other damage, similar to the way doctors use X rays to check for broken bones in their patients. Glass manufacturers need to be able to check the thickness of the glass as it is being made. Americium produces alpha radiation. The thicker the glass, the less radiation passes through. It is possible to figure out the thickness of the glass by measuring the amount of radiation that gets through.

Smoke detectors

Another important use of americium is in smoke detectors. Smoke detectors are small devices that sound an alarm if a fire starts. They are inexpensive and save lives by giving an early warning. One type, called a photoelectric detector, is activated when smoke from a fire blocks a beam of light.

The other type, called an ionization detector, contains a tiny amount of americium-241. The radioactive americium is safely sealed inside a small aluminium cylinder called an ionization chamber.

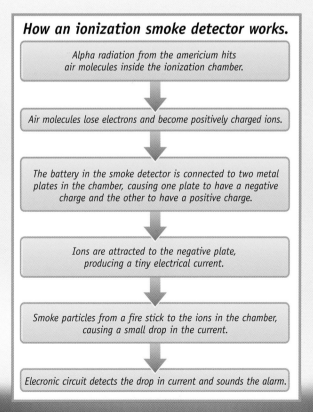

How an ionization smoke detector works.

Alpha radiation from the americium hits air molecules inside the ionization chamber.

Air molecules lose electrons and become positively charged ions.

The battery in the smoke detector is connected to two metal plates in the chamber, causing one plate to have a negative charge and the other to have a positive charge.

Ions are attracted to the negative plate, producing a tiny electrical current.

Smoke particles from a fire stick to the ions in the chamber, causing a small drop in the current.

Elecronic circuit detects the drop in current and sounds the alarm.

Curium

curium
symbol: Cm • atomic number: 96 • actinide

What does it look like?   Curium is a silvery metal that is solid at room temperature and has a density similar to mercury. This means that even small pieces are heavy. Curium reacts with water, acids, and oxygen in the air to form curium oxide. Several compounds of curium have been made, including curium chloride, $CmCl_3$, a yellow compound also called curious chloride.

Discovery of curium

Curium, the third transuranium element, was created in 1944. Helium ions were fired into some plutonium, using the cyclotron at the Lawrence Berkeley National Laboratory, in California. When Glenn Seaborg, Albert Ghiorso, and Ralph James studied this plutonium later at the University of Chicago, they discovered traces of a new element.

Curium was named after Marie and Pierre Curie, who discovered polonium and radium in the early 1900s. It is now made in several steps, which involve bombarding plutonium with neutrons. Isadore Perlman and Louis Werner first isolated pure curium metal in 1951 by reacting curium fluoride with barium metal vapor.

What are its main uses?   Curium is very radioactive and gives off alpha radiation. So much heat is generated that solutions of curium compounds may eventually boil on their own. This property has led scientists to investigate whether curium could be used as an alternative to plutonium in the radioisotope thermoelectric generators used in space probes. Unfortunately, curium also gives off powerful gamma radiation, and extra shielding would be needed to protect the people building the probe.

Curium has another important use in space probes. Both *Vega* (launched by the Soviets to Venus in 1984) and *Pathfinder* (sent to Mars by the United States in 1996) contained a device called alpha proton X ray spectrometer, which measures the amount of every element except hydrogen in rock. Curium-244 provides the alpha radiation this instrument needs to work.

▲
The probe Pathfinder *landed on Mars in 1997 and released a robotic vehicle called* Sojourner. *This photograph shows* Sojourner *analyzing a rock with a device that uses the radiation from curium.*

247 Bk berkelium 97	**berkelium**
	symbol: Bk • atomic number: 97 • actinide

Glenn Seaborg, Stanley Thompson, and Albert Ghiorso first made berkelium in 1949. Working at the Lawrence Berkeley National Laboratory, they used a cyclotron to fire helium ions at an americium target. The scientists named the new element berkelium after Berkeley, California, where the laboratory is based.

The element is now made by bombarding curium with neutrons. Several berkelium compounds have been made, including berkelium fluoride, which dissolves in water to form a green solution. At the moment, berkelium has no uses apart from scientific research. Berkelium-247 has a half-life of over 1,000 years and slowly decays to form americium again.

Californium

251 **Cf** californium 98	**californium** symbol: Cf • atomic number: 98 • actinide

Discovery of Californium

Californium was first made at the Lawrence Berkeley National Laboratory, in California, in 1950. Stanley Thompson, Kenneth Street, Albert Ghiorso, and Glenn Seaborg used a cyclotron to fire helium ions at a target containing curium. They named the new element after California.

Californium atoms are now made by bombarding plutonium with neutrons in several stages. Although metallic californium has not been isolated, several of its compounds have been made. These include californium chloride, $CfCl_3$, which dissolves in water to make a green solution. The most stable isotope is californium-251, which has a half-life of around 900 years and breaks down to form curium. However, californium-252 is a very powerful source of neutrons, and is used in neutron activation analysis. This is a method of detecting small amounts of various elements in minerals such as coal.

252 **Es** einsteinium 99	**einsteinium** symbol: Es • atomic number: 99 • actinide

The world's first hydrogen bomb was exploded at Eniwetok atoll in the Pacific Ocean on November 1, 1952. It was code named Mike, after the radio call sign for *M*, the first letter of *megaton*. The explosion produced a lot of radioactive fallout, which scientists were eager to analyze for new elements that may have been made in the explosion. Gregory Choppin, Bernard Harvey, Stanley Thompson, and Albert Ghiorso, working at the Lawrence Berkeley National Laboratory, discovered einsteinium in the fallout. At first, their discovery was kept a secret because of its connection with the hydrogen bomb.

This is the huge mushroom-shaped cloud from the world's first hydrogen bomb. Nuclear reactions during the explosion produced tiny amounts of two new elements, later called einsteinium and fermium.

The new element was named after Albert Einstein, the physicist famous for his theories on relativity. Einsteinium is now made in several stages by firing high-speed neutrons at plutonium. Little is known about its chemistry, and it is only used in research. The most stable isotope, einsteinium-252, decays to form fermium, californium, and berkelium.

257 **Fm** fermium 100	# fermium symbol: Fm • atomic number: 100 • actinide

Fermium was also discovered in 1952 in the fallout from the first hydrogen bomb's explosion by the same team that discovered einsteinium, though they also kept its discovery secret for a while. It was named in honor of Enrico Fermi, who was responsible for building the first nuclear reactor at the University of Chicago in 1942. Fermium is now made in several stages by bombarding plutonium with high-speed neutrons. Fermium-257, its most stable isotope, has a half-life of 100 days and breaks down to form californium. Some of fermium's chemistry is known, but it has no uses except for research.

Element number 100 is named after Enrico Fermi (1901–1954), seen here. Fermi was born in Italy but emigrated to the United States in 1938. His team built the world's first nuclear reactor in a makeshift laboratory under the stadium at the University of Chicago in 1942.

Mendelevium

258 **Md** mendelevium 101	**mendelevium** *symbol: Md • atomic number: 101 • actinide*

Mendelevium was first made in 1955 by Gregory Choppin, Bernard Harvey, Stanley Thompson, Albert Ghiorso, and Glenn Seaborg at the Lawrence Berkeley National Laboratory. They fired helium ions at einsteinium using a cyclotron and produced a few atoms of a new element. The scientists named it in honor of Dimitri Mendeleev, who created the first periodic table. Mendelevium is used only in research, and little is known about its chemistry. The most stable isotope, mendelevium-258, has a half-life of 51 days and decays to form einsteinium again.

This is Dimitri Mendeleev (1834–1907), the Russian chemist who developed the periodic table of elements. Mendelevium, element number 101, was named in his honor after its discovery in 1955.

259 **No** nobelium 102	**nobelium** *symbol: No • atomic number: 102 • actinide*

In 1957, a group of scientists working at the Nobel Institute of Physics in Sweden thought they had made this element. They named it after Alfred Nobel. He was the man who invented dynamite and left a legacy in his will to found the Nobel Prizes. Firing helium ions, which are relatively small particles, at metal targets, had made other transuranium elements. However, nobelium atoms are too big to be made this way, so scientists used a cyclotron to bombard curium with carbon ions. Unfortunately, it eventually turned out that they were mistaken and they had not made the new element after all.

Nobelium was reliably made for the first time in 1958 by Albert Ghiorso, Torbjorn Sikkeland, John Walton, and Glenn Seaborg working at the Lawrence Berkeley National Laboratory. They had the right to name the new element themselves because they were the discoverers, but decided to keep its name. Nobelium has no uses apart from scientific research. Its most stable isotope is nobelium-259, which has a half-life of only 58 minutes and breaks down to form mendelevium and fermium.

262 Lr lawrencium 103	**lawrencium**
	symbol: Lr • atomic number: 103 • actinide

Lawrencium was first made in 1961 at the Lawrence Berkeley National Laboratory in California by Albert Ghiorso, Torbjorn Sikkeland, Almon Larsh, and Robert Latimer. They made several isotopes of the new element by firing boron ions at high speed into a tiny amount of californium. Lawrencium was named after Ernest Lawrence, the inventor of the cyclotron. This was the machine that made the discovery of the other transuranium actinides possible, and the Lawrence Berkeley National Laboratory itself is named in his honor.

The original chemical symbol for lawrencium was Lw, but it was changed to Lr in 1965. Lawrencium has no uses outside of scientific research. Its most stable isotope is lawrencium-262, which has a half-life of just 3.6 hours, decaying to form nobelium.

◀ *Ernest Lawrence (1901– 1958) stands on a hillside overlooking the Lawrence Berkeley National Laboratory, at the University of California at Berkeley. Lawrence invented the cyclotron in 1929. Lawrencium, element number 103, is named after him.*

Find Out More About the F Block Metals

The table below contains some information about the properties of the lanthanides, the rare earth metals.

Element	Symbol	Atomic number	Melting point (°C)	Boiling point (°C)	Density (g/cm³)
Lanthanum	La	57	921	3457	6.1
Cerium	Ce	58	798	3426	6.8
Praseodymium	Pr	59	931	3512	6.6
Neodymium	Nd	60	1021	3068	7.0
Promethium	Pm	61	1168	2727	7.2
Samarium	Sm	62	1077	1791	7.5
Europium	Eu	63	822	1597	5.2
Gadolinium	Gd	64	1313	3266	7.9
Terbium	Tb	65	1356	3123	8.2
Dysprosium	Dy	66	1412	2562	8.6
Holmium	Ho	67	1474	2697	8.8
Erbium	Er	68	1529	2863	9.1
Thulium	Tm	69	1545	1947	9.3
Ytterbium	Yb	70	824	1193	7.0
Lutetium	Lu	71	1656	3395	9.8

The table below contains some information about the properties of some of the actinides. It is difficult to study the remaining eight actinides because they are transuranium elements made in tiny amounts.

Element	Symbol	Atomic number	Melting point (°C)	Boiling point (°C)	Density (g/cm³)
Actinium	Ac	89	1047	3197	10.0
Thorium	Th	90	1750	4787	11.7
Protactinium	Pa	91	1840	4027	15.4
Uranium	U	92	1132	3818	18.9
Neptunium	Np	93	640	3902	20.3
Plutonium	Pu	94	641	3232	19.8
Americium	Am	95	994	2607	13.7

Compounds

These tables show the chemical formulas of most of the compounds mentioned in this book. For example, lanthanum oxide has the formula La_2O_3. This means it is made from two lanthanum atoms and three oxygen atoms joined by chemical bonds.

Lanthanide compounds

Lanthanum compound	Formula
cerium fluoride	CeF_4
cerium nitrate	$Ce(NO_3)_4$
cerium oxide	CeO_2
dysprosium oxide	Dy_2O_3
erbium oxide	Er_2O_3
europium oxide	Eu_2O_3
gadolinium oxide	Gd_2O_3
holmium oxide	Ho_2O_3
lanthanum chloride	$LaCl_3$
lanthanum nitrate	$La(NO_3)_3$
lanthanum oxide	La_2O_3
lutetium oxyorthosilicate	Lu_2SiO_5
neodymium oxide	Nd_2O_3
praseodymium oxide	Pr_2O_3
samarium oxide	Sm_2O_3
terbium oxide	Tb_2O_3
thulium oxide	Tm_2O_3
ytterbium oxide	Yb_2O_3

Find Out More (continued)

Actinide compounds

Actinide compound	Formula
americium chloride	$AmCl_3$
americium oxide	Am_2O_3
berkelium fluoride	$BkCl_3$
curium fluoride	CmF_3
curium oxide	Cm_2O_3
curium(III) chloride	$CmCl_3$
neptunium oxide	NpO_2
plutonium oxide	PuO_2
protactinium iodide	PaI_5
protactinium oxide	Pa_2O_5
sodium diuranate	$Na_2U_2O_7$
thorium nitrate	$Th(NO_3)_4$
thorium oxide	ThO_2
thorium silicate	$ThSiO_4$
uranium ethanoate	$(CH_3COO)_2UO_2$
uranium oxide	U_3O_8
uranium tetrafluoride	UF_4
uranium(IV) oxide	UO_2
uranium(V) oxide	U_2O_5
uranium(VI) oxide	UO_3

Acids

Compound	Formula
hydrochloric acid	HCl
nitric acid	HNO_3
sulphuric acid	H_2SO_4

Other compounds

Other compounds	Formula
calcium chloride	$CaCl_2$
carbon dioxide	CO_2
carbon monoxide	CO
hydrogen fluoride	HF
magnesium fluoride	MgF_2
water	H_2O

Timeline

Element	Year	Discoverer(s)
uranium	1789	Martin Klaproth
cerium	1803	Martin Klaproth; Jöns Berzelius and Wilhem Hisinger
thorium	1828	Jöns Berzelius
lanthanum	1839	Carl Mosander
erbium	1842	Carl Mosander
terbium	1843	Carl Mosander
holmium	1878	Jacques-Louis Soret and Marc Delafontaine
ytterbium	1878	Jean de Marignac
samarium	1879	Paul-Émile Lecoq
thulium	1879	Per Teodor Cleve
gadolinium	1880	Jean de Marignac
praseodymium neodymium	1885	Carl Auer Von Welsbach
dysprosium	1886	Paul-Émile Lecoq
actinium	1899	André Debierne
europium	1901	Eugène Demarçay
lutetium	1907	Carl Auer Von Welsbach and Georges Urbain
protactinium	1913	Kasimir Fajans and Otto Göhring
neptunium	1940	Edwin McMillan and Philip Abelson
plutonium	1940	Glenn Seaborg, Edwin McMillan, Joseph Kennedy, and Arthur Wahl World's first nuclear reactor starts up
americium	1944	Glenn Seaborg, Ralph James, Leon Morgan, and Albert Ghiorso
curium	1944	Glenn Seaborg, Albert Ghiorso, and Ralph James
promethium	1945	Jack Marinsky, Lawrence Glendenin, Harold Richter, and Charles Coryell World's first uranium and plutonium bombs exploded
berkelium	1949	Glenn Seaborg, Stanley Thompson, and Albert Ghiorso
californium	1950	Stanley Thompson, Kenneth Street, Albert Ghiorso, and Glenn Seaborg
einsteinium	1952	Gregory Choppin, Bernard Harvey, Stanley Thompson, and Albert Ghiorso
fermium	1952	Gregory Choppin, Bernard Harvey, Stanley Thompson, and Albert Ghiorso World's first hydrogen bomb exploded
mendelevium	1955	Gregory Choppin, Bernard Harvey, Stanley Thompson, Albert Ghiorso, and Glenn Seaborg
nobelium	1958	Albert Ghiorso, Torbjorn Sikkeland, John Walton, and Glenn Seaborg
lawrencium	1961	Albert Ghiorso, Torbjorn Sikkeland, Almon Larshm, and Robert Latimer

Glossary

alloy mixture of two or more metals or mixture of a metal and a nonmetal

alpha radiation (∞ radiation) waves of energy caused by quickly moving helium nuclei that have broken away from an unstable nucleus

artificial not existing in nature; made by humans

atom smallest particle of an element that has the properties of that element. Atoms contain smaller particles called subatomic particles.

atomic number number of protons in the nucleus of an atom

base substance that reacts with an acid and neutralizes it. Bases that dissolve in water are also called alkalis.

beta radiation (ß radiation) waves of energy consisting of fast-moving electrons produced by an unstable nucleus when it breaks up

bond force that joins atoms together

catalyst substance that speeds up reactions without getting used up

ceramic tough solid made by heating clay and other substances to high temperatures in an oven. Plates, bathroom tiles, and toilet bowls are made from ceramics.

compound substance made from the atoms of two or more elements, joined together by chemical bonds

critical mass amount of a radioactive element needed for a chain reaction to continue at a steady rate

decay process in which the nucleus of a radioactive substance breaks up, giving off radiation and becoming the nucleus of another element

density mass of a substance compared to its volume. To find the density of a substance, you divide its mass by its volume. Substances with a high density feel very heavy for their size.

electron particle in an atom that has a negative electric charge. Electrons are found in shells around the nucleus of an atom.

element substance made from only one type of atom

extract remove a chemical from a mixture of chemicals

gamma radiation (radiation) powerful waves of energy caused by very high frequency light waves. Gamma radiation cannot be seen, and it can pass through metal.

group vertical column of elements in the periodic table. Elements in a group have similar properties.

half-life time taken for half the atoms of a radioactive substance to decay

ion charged particle made when atoms lose or gain electrons.

isotope atom of an element with the same number of protons and electrons, but a different number of neutrons. Isotopes share the same atomic number, but they have a different mass number.

mass number in the nucleus of an atom, the number of number of protons added to the number of neutrons

mineral substance that is found naturally but does not come from animals or plants. Metal ores and limestone are examples of minerals.

molecule smallest particle of an element or compound that exists by itself. A molecule is usually made from two or more atoms joined together.

neutron particle in an atom's nucleus that has no electric charge

nuclear reaction reaction involving the nucleus of an atom. Radiation is produced in nuclear reactions.

nucleus center part of an atom made from protons and neutrons. It has a positive electric charge.

ore mineral from which metals can be taken out and purified

period horizontal row of elements in the periodic table

Glossary, Continued

periodic table table in which all the known elements are arranged into groups and periods

pigment solid substance that gives color. A pigment does not dissolve in water.

proton particle in an atom's nucleur that has a positive electric charge

radiation energy or particles given off when an atom decays

radioactive producing radiation

reaction chemical change that produces new substances

refining removing impurities from a substance to make it more pure. It can also mean separating the different substances in a mixture.

subatomic particle particle smaller than an atom, such as a proton, neutron or electron

ultraviolet light invisible light just beyond the blue end of the spectrum

welding joining two or more metals together, usually by heating them

Further Reading and Useful Websites

Books

Elements. Milwaukee, Wisc.: Gareth Stevens Publishing, 2003.

Oxlade, Chris. *Elements and Compounds*. Chicago: Heinemann Library, 2002.

Oxlade, Chris. *Metals*. Chicago: Heinemann Library, 2002.

Websites

WebElementsTM
http://www.webelements.com
An interactive periodic table crammed with information and photographs.

Proton Don
http://www.funbrain.com/periodic
The fun periodic table quiz!

Mineralogy Database
http://www.webmineral.com
Lots of useful information about minerals, including colour photographs and information about their chemistry.

DiscoverySchool
http://school.discovery.com/clipartl
Help for science projects and homework, and free science clip art.

Index

actinides 7, 32–57
actinium 32, 34–35, 37–38
alloys 9, 11–12, 19, 21, 25, 28, 36
americium 32, 46, 50–51, 53
Ames process 41
atoms 5, 17, 23, 32, 35, 44, 46, 56

batteries 12
berkelium 32, 53, 55

californium 32, 54–55, 57
capacitors 26
carbon arc lamps 15
catalysts 15
catalytic converters 15
catalytic cracking 13
cathode ray tubes 22
ceramics 26
cerium 8, 14, 22, 31
cerium oxide 16
chain reactions 44
chemical symbols 35
Chenobyl 45
compounds 4–5
    lanthanide 8–9, 11, 13–16, 18, 21, 24, 26 28–29, 31
    actinide 34, 36–37, 41–43, 47, 50, 52, 54
computers 19, 22
control rods 26
critical mass 44, 48
crude oil 13
curium 32, 52
cyclotrons 46, 53, 56–57

depleted uranium 42
deuterons 48
didymia 18
DNA 33
dysprosium 26

earthquakes 30
einsteinium 32, 54–56
electron microscopy 42
electrons 5, 6 17, 23, 46
elements 4–5
enriched uranium 42
erbium 28

europium 22

fermium 32, 55, 57
fibre optic cables 28
fluorescent lamp 22–23, 25

gadolinium 24–25
gas mantles 37
glass 9, 13, 16, 18–19, 21, 28, 43, 50

half-life 20, 32–33, 38, 49, 53, 55–57
holmium 27
hydrogen bombs 46, 54–55

ions 23, 46, 48, 52, 54–57
isotopes 20, 29, 32, 38, 42, 48–49, 54–57

lanthanides 7–31
    isolation of 10–11
lanthanum 4–5, 12
lasers 9, 17, 19, 21, 27, 28–29
lawrencium 32, 57
lenses 13
light 17, 23
lutetium 31

magnets 21
magnetic resonance imaging 24
magneto-optical disc 24–25
medical imaging 31
medium source rare earth lamps 26
mendelevium 32, 56–57
minerals 9,10,18, 21, 36, 40, 54
    gadolinite 24–25, 28, 30–31
misch metal 12
missiles 36

neodymium 19
neptunium 32, 47
neutron activation analysis 54
neutrons 5, 26, 29, 32, 34–35, 44, 48, 52–54
nitrous oxides 15

nobelium 32, 56–57
nuclear fission 44, 46
    fuel 37, 42
    fusion 46
    reactors 26, 42, 45, 47–48, 55
    weapons 42, 44, 46, 48

periodic table 6, 7, 34, 47, 56
phosphors 9, 22, 25
pigments 19, 43
pitchblende 34, 38, 40
plutonium 32, 48, 55
polystyrene 15
positron emission tomography 31
praseodymium 18
promethium 9, 20
protactinium 32, 35, 38–39

radiation 31–34, 41, 46
    alpha 33, 40, 48, 50, 52–53
    beta 20, 33
    gamma 29, 33, 44, 50, 52
radioactive decay 35, 37–39, 49, 53, 55–57
radioactive waste 49
radioisotope thermoelectric generators 49
radiotherapy 33

samarium 20–21, 26
smoke detectors 50–51
space probes 49, 53
stress gauge 30

television sets 16, 19, 25
terbium 25
thorium 32, 35–39
Three Mile Island 45
thulium 29
transuranium elements 47–57
tungsten inert gas welding 36

uranium 32, 35, 38, 39,40–41, 48

yellow cake 40–41
ytterbium 30